Contents

Some words are in bold, **like this**. You can find out what they mean by looking in the glossary.

What is a kori bustard?

neck

A kori bustard is a big bird that has a long neck.

Kori bustards live alone or in small groups.

A Day in the Life: Grassland Animals

ury

Raintree

www.raintreepublishers.co.uk
Visit our website to find out more information about Raintree books.

To order:
☎ Phone 0845 6044371
▤ Fax +44 (0) 1865 312263
🖳 Email myorders@raintreepublishers.co.uk

Customers from outside the UK please telephone +44 1865 312262

Raintree is an imprint of Capstone Global Library Limited, a company incorporated in England and Wales having its registered office at 7 Pilgrim Street, London, EC4V 6LB – Registered company number: 6695582

Edited by Dan Nunn, Rebecca Rissman, Catherine Veitch and Nancy Dickmann
Designed by Philippa Jenkins
Picture research by Mica Brancic
Originated by Capstone Global Library
Printed and bound in China by South China Printing Company Ltd

ISBN 978 1 406 21899 2 (hardback)
15 14 13 12 11
10 9 8 7 6 5 4 3 2 1

ISBN 978 1 406 21903 6 (paperback)
16 15 14 13 12
10 9 8 7 6 5 4 3 2 1

British Library Cataloguing in Publication Data
Spilsbury, Louise.
Kori Bustard. -- (A day in the life. Grassland animals)
598.3'2-dc22
A full catalogue record for this book is available from the British Library.

Acknowledgements
We would like to thank the following for permission to reproduce photographs: Alamy pp. 7, 23 male (© Papilio), 17, 23 female (© AfriPics.com), 20 (© Rick Edwards ARPS), 21 (© Tim Graham); Flickr p. 16 (David Bygott); FLPA p. 12 (Malcolm Schuyl); iStockphoto pp. 4 (© Chris Wiggins), 10 (© Mike Liu), 15 (© brytta), 18, 23 jackal (© Nico Smit); Photolibrary pp. 13 (age fotostock/Nigel Dennis), 14 (Oxford Scientific (OSF)), 19 (Oxford Scientific (OSF)/Adrian Bailey); Photoshot p. 11 (© NHPA/Martin Harvey); Shutterstock pp. 5 (© Riaan van den Berg), 6, 23 crest (© Paul McKinnon), 9, 23 grassland (© Steffen Foerster Photography), 22 (© Braam Collins), 23 hyena (© Antonio Jorge Nunes), 23 insect (kd2).

Cover photograph of a close-up portrait of a kori bustard in Etosha National Park, Namibia, reproduced with permission of Shutterstock (© Johan Swanepoel). Back cover photographs of (left) the crest of a kori bustard reproduced with permission of Shutterstock (© Paul McKinnon) and (right) a kori bustard's nest reproduced with permission of Photolibrary (Oxford Scientific).

We would like to thank Michael Bright for his invaluable help in the preparation of this book.

The author would like to dedicate this book to her nephew and niece, Ben and Amelie: "I wrote these books for animal lovers like you. I hope you enjoy them." Aunty Louise.

Every effort has been made to contact copyright holders of material reproduced in this book. Any omissions will be rectified in subsequent printings if notice is given to the publisher.

All the Internet addresses (URLs) given in this book were valid at the time of going to press. However, due to the dynamic nature of the Internet, some addresses may have changed, or sites may have changed or ceased to exist since publication. While the author and publisher regret any inconvenience this may cause readers, no responsibility for any such changes can be accepted by either the author or the publisher.

Kori bustards can fly, but they do not fly much because they are so heavy.

They spend most days and nights on the ground.

What do kori bustards look like?

crest

A kori bustard has a grey neck, and black and white shoulders.

It has a black **crest** and a white stripe over each eye.

An adult **male** kori bustard weighs about the same as a four-year-old boy!

A **female** is much smaller than a male.

Where do kori bustards live?

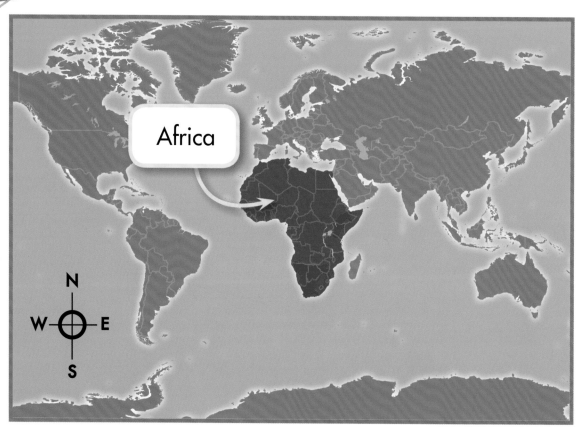

Africa

key: ▪ = where kori bustards live

Kori bustards live in parts of southern and eastern Africa.

They mostly live in places called **grasslands**.

In these grasslands the land is covered in grasses and a few trees.

Most days it is hot and dry, but in some months it rains a lot.

What do kori bustards do during the day?

Kori bustards look for food in the mornings and afternoons.

At midday when it gets very hot, they rest in a shady spot.

Kori bustards often feed near zebras.

When zebras walk they bring out small animals that kori bustards like to eat.

What do kori bustards eat?

snake

Kori bustards eat insects and small animals, like mice and snakes.

Sometimes they eat seeds and berries too.

Kori bustards get water from the food they eat.

They also drink from pools of water that fill up during the rainy months.

Where do kori bustards lay eggs?

nest

Female kori bustards scrape a shallow pit between grasses for a nest.

This keeps the eggs cool and hidden during the day.

Mothers stay with the eggs day and night.

They throw grass onto their backs so other animals cannot see them.

What are kori bustard chicks like?

Chicks are striped so they are hard to see among grasses in the day.

They eat **insects** that their mothers catch for them.

During the day, a chick often walks in its mother's shadow.

This keeps it out of the heat.

Which animals hunt kori bustards?

jackal

Big animals like **jackals**, eagles, **hyenas**, and lions hunt kori bustards.

When kori bustards are scared, they bark or growl.

Sometimes small birds sit on a kori bustard's back eating **insects**.

They warn kori bustards when danger is near because they suddenly fly off!

What do kori bustards do at night?

In the evening, kori bustards find a safe place in long grass.

They use their beak to clean their feathers carefully.

When it is dark, kori bustards lay down for the night.

Most kori bustards sleep alone, but chicks sleep next to their mothers.

Kori bustard body map

beak

crest

back

neck

leg

Glossary

crest feathers that stick up on some birds' heads

female animal that can become a mother when it is grown up

grassland land where mostly grasses grow

hyena wild animal that mostly lives in grasslands in Africa. It looks like a dog.

insect small animal with six legs. Ants, beetles, and bees are insects.

jackal wild animal that lives in Africa and Asia. It looks like a dog or a fox.

male animal that can become a father when it is grown up

Find out more

Books

Amazing Animals of South Africa, Dawid Van Lill
(LAPA, 2007)

Birds (Classifying Animals), Sarah Wilkes
(Wayland, 2007)

Websites

http://koribustardssp.org/Home_Page.php
http://www.arkive.org/kori-bustard/ardeotis-kori/info.html

Index